BRAINTICKLERS® II

W9-AKX-375

QUESTIONS FOR CEOs
ELIZABETH ARNOLD & ROD BECKSTRÖM with TOM STAUFFER
Young Presidents' Organization

Brainticklers® Publishing
1705 14th St., Suite 136
Boulder, CO 80302
Tel: 303-247-1539
Web: www.brainticklers.com

Printed in the United States of America

ISBN 0-9675731-1-4

Cover Illustration: Dick Truxaw
Cover Design: Jill Ziegler

The Library of Congress Cataloging-in-Publication Data available upon request

Arnold, Elizabeth
Beckström, Rod

"This book will save you millions in consulting fees. Put one by your bed, on your desk and in the bathroom. This is the job description for CEO's and CEO wannabes."

—Peter Jackson
CEO
Intraware, Inc.

"The most important job of a CEO is to ask the right questions. This book gives each of us a great start with so many enjoyable, engaging and challenging questions for our businesses and our lives."

—J. David Martin
International President 2001-2002
Young Presidents Organization
Chairman, The Martin Group

Acknowledgments

We thank our loved ones for sharing their inspiration and light. We thank our friends and colleagues who tickled our brains about this project, especially Eva Sonesh-Kedar, Tim Draper, Pete Estler, David Martin, Chris Anderson, Ed Barbera, John and Kara Arnold, Terry Healey, Sharon Harston and Kathy Smith. As always, Kim Carlisle of Literatae provided valuable insights and kept our p's and q's in line, and Jill Zeigler and Diana Trott dressed our questions in an elegant design. Last but first, we thank each of you for asking yourself questions about your life. You are our heroes.

Elizabeth Arnold, Rod Beckström and Tom Stauffer

Table of Contents

Introduction

BRAINTICKLERS® for CEOs

Bigger, higher, stronger. New models. Old models. Role models. Global markets. Round-the-clock service. Greater expectations. Broader visibility. More information faster and faster. Less and less time.

As we catapult into this new century, the pressure on CEOs, their companies and families has never been greater.

Yet, last time we checked, CEOs are still human. They love, fear, seek joy and get angry. They have lives, dreams and hopes outside of work. They have loved ones with whom they want to spend time. They need to sleep, eat and move.

In the midst of these often-conflicting demands, how does a CEO handle the pressure? How does he or she sustain the pace? Find or maintain inner peace?

Sure, we could have written a book of answers. We could have told you our theories of creating success, joy, and the perfect life. But we felt this would miss the point.

We recognize that you and you alone know what is best for you. Only you know where you are in your life today and where you want to be. Besides, this book is written by CEOs for CEOs, those who plan to be CEOs and those who love them. We all know how well *we* take directions from others.

We believe nothing changes until we ask ourselves questions. Our hope is to spark your creativity and intellect by sharing some thought-provoking questions. Questions automatically jump start thoughts. Our neurons can't help it. Thoughts produce actions.

Each of us may choose when and how we respond to the insights we uncover as we explore the answers, but we will respond in some way at some point. Guaranteed.

So, want to change your life? Want to improve your business? Or just get more sleep? The best answers for each of us start with questions.

BRAINTICKLERS®

Elizabeth Arnold and Rod Beckström created BRAINTICKLERS to stimulate creative thought about how we live our lives today by asking questions. For more information on the BRAINTICKLERS series, please visit **www.brainticklers.com** or contact us at:

BRAINTICKLERS®
1705 14th Street, Suite 136
Boulder, CO 80302
(303) 247-1539

When we decided to write a book for CEOs,
we knew whom to call…

The Young Presidents Organization

Few other organizations provide more value to CEOs than YPO.
For over 50 years YPO has prepared "better presidents through
education and idea exchange." We authors have experienced first-
hand how strongly YPO fulfills its mission.

In addition, the more than 8,000 CEO members of YPO worldwide provide a bellwether for all CEOs and those who aspire to
join their ranks. Although they operate in different cultures, YPO
members face similar questions. Because they are all under 50
years of age, they are part of the world's emerging dynamic leadership. Together YPO members represent trillions of dollars in
economic activity that is helping to shape world business and
many other avenues of professional activity.

For more information on YPO, please visit **www.ypo.org**.

I. Leadership

1. What business leader inspires you most? What business leader are you most like?

2. What leadership lessons does Mother Theresa provide us? Nelson Mandella? Bill Clinton? Why?

3. Who's your guru — Tom Peters,
   Peter Drucker or Mahatma Ghandi?
   Why?

4. Which results in better CEO leadership — a warrior work ethic, charisma, team-building talent or vision?

5. What is the best preparation to be a CEO — liberal arts education, parenting, technical expertise, marketing skill or something else?

6. Is leadership exhibited best by personal example or company performance? Will your legacy be measured by your leadership qualities, corporate results, strategic positioning, investor satisfaction or ethical behavior?

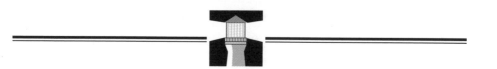

7. Would you rather revolutionize your industry or crush your competition?

8. Do you lead by fear or inspiration? How do you know? Do you reward your employees more for obedience or innovation?

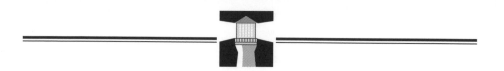

9. How would you like your daughter's boss to treat her? Your son's boss to treat him? How do you treat your employees?

10. In your industry does a CEO best serve his or her company by maintaining distance from employees or by getting involved with them directly?

11. Who in your organization has the courage to challenge you? How do they impact your performance? Will you promote them or shove them in a corner?

12. When a CEO's leadership flags, what is the best source of help? What early warning systems can a CEO put in place to gauge when exhaustion takes a toll on performance?

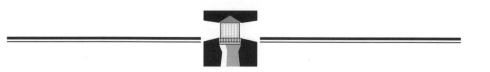

13. How does your personal stress level impact your company?

14. In what areas have you worked more and produced less? Where has your working less produced more?

15. How comfortable are you with conflict? Do you avoid it or manage it? How does your comfort level with conflict affect your leadership style? Your interpersonal communications?

16. What do your employees know
    about you? How do they rate you?
    Do you care?

17. Do you trust consultants? Under
what conditions would you hire
them? Why do CEOs hire
management consultants if they then
dismiss the consultants' advice as
useless or ignore their conclusions?

18. How differently might younger and older CEOs view the importance of knowledge management, finance and client service?

19. How safe are your products and
your company's workplace?
How should these metrics fit into
your performance evaluation?

20. When did you last reinvent your company? When did you last reinvent yourself?

21. Given that almost all world faiths
    support the idea that we should
    treat others as we would like to be
    treated, how do you translate this
    insight into your business?

22. Have you interviewed any 80-year-old retired business leaders for their wisdom and advice?

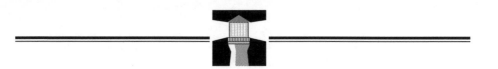

23. What are some of the myths about you as a leader? What is the actual reality?

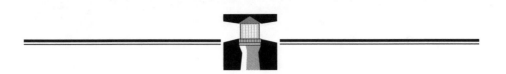

24. How much do you listen? How
    much do you tell?

25. How does your leadership style now differ from your leadership style when you first began your career?

26. On what assumptions do you base your leadership style? Are these assumptions true? What untested hypotheses do you have in your mind about the way you run your business?

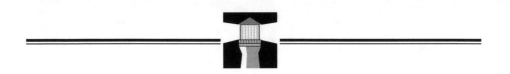

27. What would you most like to change about your leadership style? What's stopping you from changing it?

II. Corporate Culture

1. What expressions do your
   employees wear as they enter work?
   Do they frown or smile, walk quickly
   or slowly, hunch up their shoulders
   or relax? What do you do?

2. Is your company a play zone where innovation can thrive or is it a creativity death zone?

3. What happens to people who come up with great ideas in your company? What happens to people who make a mistake? Do you really encourage risk taking or do you scare people away from it?

4. What are the core values of your company? How do they relate to the values of your customers?

5. Think of three people in your company. Why do they work for you? What responsibility do you feel toward them?

6. Does the 25-year-old computer guy in your company think that you get it? What about the forklift operator or the customer service representative who handles complaints?

7. What do you expect from your
   employees — great things or
   hassles? What do you get?

8. What are the archetypes of your company? White knight? Alchemist? Bully? Magician? Loyal servant?

9. How many of your employees are addicted to destructive drugs? Alcohol? Are you? What do you do about it?

10. In your company, what groups socialize together outside work? Are women, minorities and other traditionally marginalized groups involved?

11. How comfortable are you with the ethnic and gender diversity of your workplace? How many women and minorities are executives in your company?

12. How many hours do you sleep each week? What about your company's key managers? Research and development crew? Marketing professionals?

13. Do your managers press for or evoke results?

14. How stressed out are you and your
    employees? How do you help them
    manage stress?

15. What is the ratio of your salary to the lowest compensation paid to an employee? Who has access to salary and performance metrics in the company?

16. How does your employee benefit package incent behavior that furthers your corporate mission? What input do your employees have into their benefits packages?

17. Besides financial support and health
plans, what can you contribute to
your employees' lives?

18. What song best describes your company?

19. How many conversations do you start by thanking someone for something great they have done?

20. When you speak to your employees, do you speak to their hearts, their minds or their guts?

21. How many savvy, open-minded,
talented twenty-year olds think your
company is a cool place to work?

22. Do your employees feel respected
    and valued by you and the company?
    Are they proud to work at your
    company? How do you know?

III. Business Basics

1. Which is more important for your enterprise — cash, profitability or perceived growth?

2. How sustainable are the raw
   materials and resources used in your
   company? Can you convert to a
   more sustainable source?

3. What deadwood stands in your forest? What unnourished seedlings?

4. Which is a better strategy for your business development — conflict or strategic cooperation?

5. What can you do to create the best business game of the century and have your company win it?

6. How can you revolutionize your
   industry? How can you exercise
   influence beyond your industry?

7. Is the "new economy" real, or is it
   just business jargon? If it is real, what
   parts of it are already old? What
   does it mean for your business?

8. What business model does your company most resemble — a shark, a cow or a banana (growing by eating smaller companies, grazing on mature markets, or manufacturing a basic product from multiple natural resources)?

9. What are the five biggest challenges your industry faces in the next ten years? What can you do today to turn these into opportunities for your business?

10. What are the top five most likely public relations crises your company might face? What can you do today to prevent them? To prepare for them?

11. What is your five-second elevator
pitch? Can you articulate your
business model on one page or less?
Have you done it?

12. What current financial metrics for your company can you state off the top of your head? Which ones should you know but don't? Who in your company does?

13. If your budget were slashed by 30%, how would your company get the same things done?

14. Do you understand the implications of hedging for your business? What does risk management mean to you? Volatility?

15. When was the last time you called
    your company and pretended to be
    a customer?

16. How much time do you spend with your key customers each week? Month? Year? What three words do they most often use to describe your product or services?

17. When your company does not
    appear on the list of "best companies
    to work for," how do you respond?

18. Do you trust your employees?
    Do they trust you? How do you
    know?

19. Which is more important to you —
your vice presidents or your
personal assistant? How differently
are they compensated?

20. How well does your team play ball together? If you were temporarily unable to communicate with them, how would things get done?

21. What is your future with your company? Do you have a business exit strategy? A personal one?

22. What is the best possible future you
can imagine for your company?
For your employees? For you?

IV. Technology

1. How might changes in technology force changes in your business model? How risky are your assumptions?

2. How are your competitors using technology to reinvent their businesses and operating models? What are the implications for you?

3. How can technology triple your company's productivity over the next five or ten years? How might you invent new technology to make this happen as cost effectively as possible?

4. Have you made business decisions because you did not want to appear behind the times in technology even though the decisions violated basic business principles? What were the results?

5. Is technology increasing stress at your company or helping people live more flexible, balanced lives?

6. Do you use the information technology yourself that you insist others use in the company?

7. Would you put GPS tracking systems in your company's vehicles if you had to have one in your own car?

8. When you or your employees surf
   the web, do you know who watches
   your movements, or how?
   Do you care?

9. What information do you believe
   companies have the right to keep
   about their clients? With whom can
   they share this information?

10. What moral questions would you consider before introducing organic robots into your company?

11. If we could engineer the ideal
lifespan, how long would it be?

12. What is your greatest hope for
    information technology?
    Your greatest fear?

V. World

1. Which more potently shapes national economies — forces of globalization in trade or the economic policies of individual nations?

2. What is the next biggest worldwide trend after economic globalization and information technology? How will it impact your business?

3. Now that many multinational
   corporations operate like
   independent nation states, how have
   CEOs of multinationals become
   more like heads of state?

4. Has the 250% increase in the number of nations in the world in the last 50 years harmed or helped world peace and stability? If the number of nations doubles in the next 50 years, how will world order be affected?

5. If you were Prime Minister of China, what would top your liberalization agenda?

6. What percentage of the human population benefits from global free trade and capitalism?

7. How does globalization impact the digital divide?

8. Does the spread of a world culture through TV, Internet and movies increase cross-cultural understanding and economic demand or envy and violence?

9. How best can nations preserve their
   heritage in the face of this spreading
   world culture?

10. If economic sanctions buttress abusive dictators, why and when should a nation use them?

11. If you were the ruler of an island nation forecasted to be flooded by rising seas resulting from global warming, what would you do? Who should be held responsible?

12. What is your governments' ratio of military arms to national education expenditures?

13. What explains the apparent economic differences between the North and South in world economic performance? Why are some nations poor and others rich?

14. One sixth of the world survives on $1/day or less. What responsibility do business leaders have to help reduce poverty?

15. How many currencies are needed worldwide? How many nations? Why?

16. Who benefits most when countries dollarize?

17. Is English now the global language of business and science? Will another language overtake it?

18. How best can a CEO (or future CEO) gain the global understanding necessary to run a multinational company — multiple foreign postings, long hours at corporate headquarters, extensive travel?

19. How sympathetic are you to other cultures? Have you ever attended religious services of another faith?

20. In recent years more than thirty wars have raged simultaneously. Will global economic forces dampen or encourage such violence in years to come?

21. Which nations will be the
    superpowers in 100 years? 500?

VI. Ethics

1. What moral compromises are you willing to make to win the next big deal? Where do you draw the line?

2. If you could close a deal by providing a client an evening with private dancers, would you? How would you feel if your son or daughter showed up as one of the dancers?

3. What is the fine line between wining, dining, golfing, entertaining and bribing?

4. Which is more likely to encourage corporate social responsibility — tax breaks or pressure for a positive public image? In this time of fast information transfer, is social responsibility simply good business strategy?

5. If you ran a shipping line and learn that flushing your bilges may internationally spread species that destroy local habitats, how much would you spend to prevent such destruction in the absence of government regulation?

6. If you ran a biotechnology company, what might you deem too risky for society to develop? Organic machines? Genetically altered products which might have unknown side effects?

7. If genetic engineering might prolong your life by ten years and steadily increase economic growth but pose huge social and environmental risks, would you proceed?

8. If you could ask job applicants for volunteer DNA data that might save you major insurance costs, would you? What are your thoughts on toilet bowl technology that could read DNA and test for drugs from urine in workplace bathrooms?

9. Where can CEOs focus their
   humanitarian efforts most efficiently
   — at home in their own
   communities or throughout the
   world?

10. If half of all living species might disappear in the next one hundred years, what should you do to alter that outcome? Should we deduct their value from our global gross product? How should we value each species?

11. What special responsibilities, if any, do traditional business figures have at a time when business leaders can receive celebrity attention?

12. What privacy rights should people have? Your employees? Your family?

13. If you could enter a contract tomorrow in which you were assured a $20 million personal profit over three years' time but your gut told you not to do it, what would you do?

14. Why does crime so closely correlate to poverty? Which should be attacked first?

15. How should society determine which drugs it makes illegal?

16. Given the studies that link watching TV violence and committing violent acts, where do you spend your advertising dollars?

17. What social values are reflected in
your company's performance
metrics? Environmental goals?
Employee development goals?
Social contribution?

18. How does your firm practice charity? As a marketing tool? To help expand your CEO's ego? To back employee beliefs? To contribute to a better world?

19. If your employees were to rate your company's business and professional ethics, how would they rate them on a scale of 1 to 10?

20. If all six billion humans lived your
    lifestyle, how would the planet react?

21. What kind of life do you wish for your great, great grandchildren in terms of the right balance between environment and wealth? How are you helping to create that world?

VII. Sex, Money and Power

1. Where do you get your energy —
   adrenaline, love, conflict, sex, health,
   recognition, joy, coffee?

2. If asked, "What can you do today
   that will blow your partner's mind?"
   do you think of buying lunch,
   cooking dinner or having sex?

3. How many sexual partners have you had in the past year? How many people did you think about having sex with today? What influences these numbers?

4. Can you have a meeting with an attractive person without thinking about sex? What do you do differently when you negotiate with women than when you negotiate with men? Is it easier? More difficult?

5. How does your work show up in the sex you have? How does the sex you have (or don't) show up in your work?

6. Do you prefer to be on the top or bottom when you draw your organizational charts?

7. What would employees cite as the glass ceiling in your company?

8. To whom are you most attracted — people most like you, people who challenge you, people who enhance your self-image or people who teach you?

9. What scares you most in business?
In other areas of your life? How are
these similar? If you didn't have these
fears, how would you operate
differently?

10. To what power at home does your income entitle you? Does your spouse have full information about your finances? How are spending decisions made in your household?

11. Would you find your spouse/partner more or less attractive to you if he/she made more money than you? Had more fame?

12. If someone on your key management team has to stay late on Friday to take a conference call and you have a family but another officer does not, who stays? Why?

13. Imagine you have just sold the company you founded for $200 million. How do you feel without CEO responsibilities?

14. When do you feel most powerful?
Least powerful?

15. How much money do you really
need? If you had that much, what
would you do?

16. What makes you burn with envy?
What can you learn from it?

17. Which would you choose — tripling your personal wealth or fifty years of global peace?

VIII. Family

1. How do the economics of love differ from the economics of investment?

2. What requires greater management skills and stamina — providing primary care for three future teenagers or storming a new market? Why are the money and power associated with these two choices so disparate?

3. How stable and loving is your children's environment? Are they able to be kids, or must they function as little adults?

4. What does money symbolize to your children — hard work, power, toys, opportunity, education?

5. What are your spouse's/partner's wildest dreams? Biggest fears? What are those of your children?

6. How happy is your spouse/partner in your relationship? Have you asked him or her recently? What is your customer service plan in this department?

7. When was the last time you and
   your spouse/partner had a date?

8. How is your relationship with your parents? What do you want it to be?

9. Does your family have a vision for the future and a code of conduct to which all members agree?

10. What is the best way you can contribute to your family — money, time, being a role model? What do they receive from you on a daily basis?

11. What are the five biggest risks your family faces? What are your family's five biggest opportunities? How can you prepare for these?

12. What do your loved ones most
    adore about you? What do you love
    most about yourself?

13. Are your children afraid of you?
Is your spouse? Do you want them
to be?

14. Have the Internet, cell phones and other technology helped or harmed relations within your family?

15. In which century are your family's values and practices based — 19th, 20th or 21st? Should that change?

16. What is the most effective strategy for you to balance work and family — compartmentalization, integration, something else?

17. How do your kids talk about your
company? How does your spouse?

18. When did you last take your spouse/partner or children on a business trip? Did it work?

IX. Play

1. What do you do for fun?

2. If you chucked your business and became a musician, what instrument would you play? In what band?

3. What makes you laugh? When was the last time you laughed so hard that your belly shook?

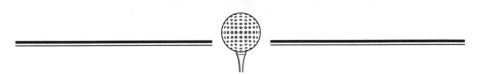

4. What silly thing can you do today just for fun?

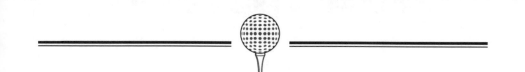

5. When was the last time you had a
day with no agenda?

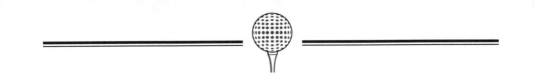

6. How do you fuel your creativity?

7. Do you have any games or gizmos in your office? Does your company have a VP of Fun?

8. Do you tend to pick subordinates who are more serious in demeanor or those who are more flexible and appear to be having more fun in their lives?

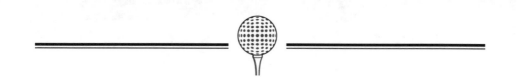

9. What rocks your world?

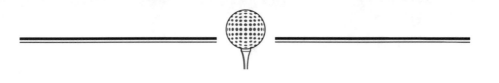

10. Who are your play buddies?

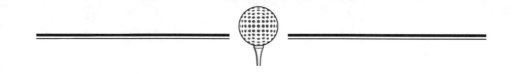

11. Why is this the shortest chapter in this book?

X. Self

1. When you step outside in the morning, do you expect a hostile or loving world? What do you find?

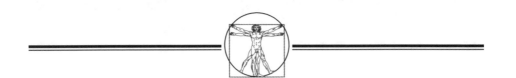

2. When challenges cross your path,
   to what or to whom do you turn?
   What are you seeking there?
   How consistently do you find it?

3. When things don't go your way,
   whom do you blame? Why?

4. What unmet needs at home do you
   try to meet through your work?
   What unmet needs at work do you
   try to meet at home?

5. How stressed do you feel? Who or what prevents you from bringing balance to your life?

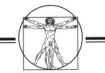

6. Do you have a mission statement for your life? A five-year plan? Or do you simply live in the present moment?

7. How would you describe yourself to someone without referring to your business, family, possessions or associations?

8. How high is your emotional intelligence quotient — empathizing with others, withholding gratification, keeping your word, etc.? Would others agree? What can you do to raise it?

9. What does your dream life look like?
   Given the wealth of resources at
   your disposal, what keeps you from
   creating it?

10. How can you make your job nourish
your spirit?

11. If you were to die in five years, how would you spend the time between now and then? Five days? Five minutes?

12. If your great-grandmother saw you today, what advice might she share with you? Your great-grandfather?

13. What kind of grandparent do you want to be?

14. Who are the three happiest people you know? Why are they so happy? How do they affect the people around them?

15. With whom in the world can you share your deepest, innermost thoughts? When do you bare your soul to another?

16. At whom are you most angry in your life? Can you forgive them? Yourself?

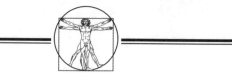

17. What ten things bring you the most pleasure? How sustainable and healthy are these?

18. What music moves you most deeply?
    How often do you listen to it?

19. What happens to your heart rate
    when you turn off your cell phone?
    What happens to your self-esteem?

20. How disciplined are you? How disciplined do you want to be? Are you disciplined out of need, desire or fear?

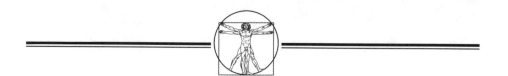

21. How limber is your mind? Your
    body? How are they related?

22. How open is the dialogue between your logic and your emotions?

23. When have you found your intuition
to be right on? When have you
found your intuition to be off base?
What happened then?

24. What is the wildest, most creative thing you would like to do in your remaining business years? Your life?

25. Do you have an ethical will which sets out how you would like the values important to you to be passed on?

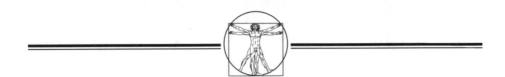

26. What do you do personally to prevent a heart attack or other stress-related disease?

27. What drove you to be a CEO?
    What drives you now?

28. How different is your public self
from your private self?

29. What do you want people to say about you in your eulogy?

30. Why is this the longest chapter in
this book?

XI. Spirituality

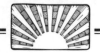

1. What are the greatest lessons
   Ghandi, Martin Luther King and
   Lao Tzu have given us? What are the
   greatest lessons Morgan, Rockefeller
   and Gates have given us?

2. What large corporation has the
   highest level of integrity?

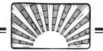

3. What does spirituality mean to you?
Who is your spiritual hero?

4. If Jesus, Mohammed, Solomon, Krishna or Buddha were running your company, what changes would he make?

5. If you could ask one religious figure to visit you, whom would you invite? What questions would you most like to ask him or her?

6. Some religions maintain that God created humans in God's image. What precisely does this mean to you in terms of your self-worth? The worth of those around you?

7. If humans are intelligent probes
   created by God so God could
   experience this creation from
   billions of different perspectives,
   do you feel belittled or blessed?

8. Will a time come when people do not kill one another in the name of religion?

9. Given that Einstein taught us that space and time are relative and spiritual leaders tell us time does not exist in the spiritual world, how can you incorporate timeless meaning into your life?

10. Who or what fixed the speed of light? Is love faster?

11. What does unconditional love mean
to you? How often do you give it?
Receive it?

12. What are the most inspiring words you have ever heard?

13. What is your greatest gift? How does it serve others — family, friends, etc.?

14. If you still your mind and listen to your heart, what does the quietest voice inside you say?

15. How open is your mind?

16. If God instructed you to quit your current job and wait in silence for three months for your next guidance, would you?

17. What makes God laugh? Does he or she have a gender?

18. What is the biggest fib you have ever told in business?

19. What is your greatest wish for the world?

About the Authors

Elizabeth Arnold
is an executive coach, facilitator and speaker (**www.coacharnold.com**) who works with CEOs, entrepreneurs and their families. A former YPO'er and an entrepreneur since age 11, Elizabeth's ventures have been diverse. She has served as CEO/President and founder/CEO of several companies; as a corporate, estate and tax attorney; and as a strategic consultant. She is also a published author. Elizabeth received her BA Summa Cum Laude from Yale, her JD from Harvard, her LLM in Tax from NYU and her boiler mechanic certification from PPA.

Rod Beckström
is Co-Chairman of NConfidence.com (**www.nconfidence.com**), Director of American Legal Net, Trustee of the Environmental Defense Fund (**www.edf.org**), and was founder, Chairman and CEO of CATS Software Inc. which he helped build from garage to public company to sale. He is Chairman of the Golden Gate Chapter of the Young Presidents' Organization, founding partner of Silicon Valley Social Venture and is a member of the Band of Angels. He received his BA and MBA from Stanford University and was a Fulbright Scholar.

Tom Stauffer
is Chief Executive Officer of Young Presidents' Organization International (**www.ypo.org**), a 51-year-old worldwide forum for CEOs under the age of 50. Previously, he has served as president of two American universities and worked for NASA and the American Council on Education. He has lectured at dozens of institutions, has well over 100 books and articles to his credit and has chaired more than a dozen civic organizations. His PhD is from the Graduate School of International Studies, University of Denver, where he was named distinguished alumnus.